This book belongs to

Monica & And Women

Who, seek the Lord's Beauty

I N G *a woman beautiful*

Their *in God's eyes.*

lives

GROWTH AND STUDY GUIDE

Beautiful in God's Eyes

Elizabeth George

HARVEST HOUSE PUBLISHERS

EUGENE, OREGON

Cover by Terry Dugan Design, Minneapolis, Minnesota

Acknowledgment

As always, thank you to my dear husband, Jim George, M.Div.,Th.M., for your able assistance, guidance, suggestions and loving encouragement on this project.

BEAUTIFUL IN GOD'S EYES GROWTH AND STUDY GUIDE

Contents

A Word of Welcome

~o~

*W*elcome to this helpful and practical handbook for you and others who desire to become even more beautiful in God's eyes. The book *Beautiful in God's Eyes* and this growth and study guide highlight the 22 excellent character qualities for women presented in Proverbs 31:10-31. No matter what your age, stage, or marital status, your journey verse-by-verse through this passage in the Bible will be relevant and motivating!

A Word of Instruction

The exercises in this study guide center on the Bible and are easy to do. You'll need your copy of the book *Beautiful in God's Eyes*, your Bible, a dictionary, and a heart ready to discover what God has to say to you about becoming a woman of authentic beauty.

In each lesson you'll be asked to read the corresponding chapter from *Beautiful in God's Eyes* and answer questions that will help you better understand God's plan and purpose for you as a woman. The aim of this study is to fine-tune your knowledge of God's design for your heart and your life—both inside and out—and to help you apply God's truth in life-changing ways.

A Word for Your Group

You will grow as you work your way through the biblical principles presented in this study guide and use them in daily life. But I urge you to share the rich and life-changing journey with others—with your friends, with a small group of neighbors, with the women in your Sunday school class or Bible study. In a group, no matter how small or large, there is personal care and interest. There is sharing. There are sisters-in-Christ to pray for you. There is a mutual exchange of experiences. There is accountability. And, yes, there is peer pressure, which helps us get our lessons done so that glorious growth occurs! And there is sweet, sweet encouragement as you share God's Word with others and stimulate one another to greater love and good works.

To encourage you to organize and lead a group, I've included a section titled "Leading a Bible Study Discussion Group." You may also find this information and more on my website, **www.ElizabethGeorge.com**.

A Word of Encouragement

As you daily incorporate the truths from God's Word that are featured in the book *Beautiful in God's Eyes* and in this exciting study guide, you will never be the same! By God's grace and with His help, you will find yourself being transformed day-by-day into the woman you yearn to be—a woman who reflects God's nature, lives out His goals, brings honor and glory to His name, and blesses others—a woman who is truly beautiful in God's eyes.

In His great and everlasting love,

Elizabeth George

-1-

A Rare Treasure
Her Character

Read the chapter in *Beautiful in God's Eyes* titled "A Rare Treasure—Her Character." How did this chapter encourage you?

This chapter encouraged me in so many ways, I belive that if the Lord made such an amazing women to follow after. I belive that I can be that women. Because God wants each of his women to hae

How did it challenge you?

In my opionion. This challanged me Quit a bit. I thougnt Lord how am I going to have these Qualities? How am I going to grow like this women.

What ideas were new to you or showed you an area you need to pay more attention to?

At first all I can think about Was, Does this women really exsit? The one idea I fellt was new to me was that this women wasn't Born like this but over time she was able to rise to be the women God has called her to be

All this charac

An Alphabet of Character

Read through Proverbs 31:10-31, God's portrait of the kind of woman who is beautiful in His eyes. Jot down the character traits you see in her.

Value far beyond pearls, trusting, brings Good not Evil, Hard workes, Wise, Strong, successful, Giving, Does not worry about what tomorrow may hold. married a Good man. Dignity, Kind, her family adores her.

Why do you think this portrait is in the Bible?

I belive that this women models Godly living in Every area of her life. This women is a Great example That our Lord gives us, to become like this women. To be what he really Created us to be.

Which is your favorite verse and why?

my favorite verse is Prov. 31:30 - "Charm is deceptive and beauty is fleeing but a women who fears the Lord shall be praised" this ves says it all. If we fear the Lord, and love him Then, Nothing Else matters -

Which is the most challenging verse to you and why?

The most challenging to me would be 10-31. It is very difficult to have all these Characteristic, it is going to be a Challenge, but I know that through Christ Jesus it will all work out!

A Picture of Beauty

Look up the word "virtuous" (or worthy, excellent, noble, capable, whichever term your Bible uses in Proverbs 31:10) in a dictionary and write out a simple definition. (As a bonus, you can look up all of the terms above!)

"Worthiny" A women who is Deserving to have good things. to do do Good things in her life according to God.

The word "virtuous" (worthy, excellent, noble, capable, well) is used only four times in the Bible to describe a woman. Read these verses and note why each woman merits this description.

Ruth 3:11—This women was led to follow her mother-law because of her great love for her. She is a compassionate women!

Proverbs 12:4 (KJV)—This women, is loved by her husbend, becose she is a Good women. There for her husbend adores her

Proverbs 31:10—This is a women Of Great virtue— a Good man Seeks this kind of women for She has allowed God to do a work in her!

Proverbs 31:29 (KJV)—

meaning —that women hae be Proen to do well but this women Goes beyond the Surface, This women is being / allowed to be Prefected by her Lord.

A *powerful mind*—Think about your life for a moment. When do you need power of mind to endure and follow-through?

I would have to say in my day dd life - IN decisions, making, I know that I must Go to God for all the Answers to my days problems.

What can you do today to strengthen yourself in this area? Pray about it now—and take a first step! What will it be?

I must not take it upon my Self to make decisions without my Lord - to to give him every Area Of my life - For he only knows what's ahead.

A *powerful body*—Now think about your body. When do you need power of body to endure and follow-through?

I would say to find meaning IN my life - TO allow the Lord to take over - TO Set Goals - and to achieve them.

What can you do today to strengthen yourself in this area? Pray about it now. What will your first step be?

Lord help me to Give my life to to you! I need to let Go of self - to have you Guide me Daily - to find fullment IN you Amen.

An Army of Virtues

What is your response to being pictured as a "soldier" or "warrior" when it comes to your many roles and responsibilities?

Some times I feel that everything lies on me- I feel I am being stretched in all directions in life. One day- I feel like a soldier who must stay strong through lifes battles, and other times I feel like a "warrior" that with christ I can Get through lifes battles.

How do you measure up?

I know that without the lord I can't accomplish anything. And so I do not measure up well, I need to be and feel like my lord wants me in the front lines, so that I may come at strong in the End-

Can you think of changes that need to be made? List several of the "big ones" here.

① TO trust in the lord- "faith" Not by sight"
② Strength in the lord to get through battles, Boldness, to speak what the lord has for me

The How-To's of Beauty

1. *Cultivate the desire*—List four or five desires you would like to realize by the end of your life.

   Virtue, Bold, Noble, worthy

   What can you do in at least one of those areas of desire...

   Today? Noble, to be good to others, to help others

   This week?
   to help those who are in need.

2. *Give it time*—What steps can you take today to ensure you have time for each of these areas?

   Time reading God's Word—
   To take 5 minutes and stand reading God's word

   Time with other godly women—

   Time reading biographies—

An Invitation to Beauty

The Proverbs 31 woman didn't just happen. She didn't just appear overnight. No, she grew and developed as God worked in her heart and life...one day at a time...over a lifetime. Do you desire to be this kind of woman? Then write out a short prayer of commitment to God describing your desire and ask Him for His strength for today...and for a lifetime...as His Proverbs 31 woman.

Lord, my desire is to be this women of Prov 31. Help work in my daily to life to reach this Goal - rise me Lord to be this women - make me Lord the women of your desire - I love you lord with all of my heart and soul, bless me Jesus men.

My Prayer of Commitment

Lord of all beauty and grace,
help me to remember to improve or change
this one thing in my life: *TO*

Eat your word more!!

-2-

A Sparkling Jewel
Her Value

Read the chapter in *Beautiful in God's Eyes* titled "A Sparkling Jewel—Her Value." How did this chapter encourage you?

Being Beautiful, is Not real Outside beauty - The beauty the Lord is Speaking of is within - A Jewel, must be worked on, it doesn't Necessey happen over night, It is the outmost encouragement to know that our Lord is Patient with US.

How did it challenge you?

It is a great struggle, to see that a women with all Characteristic virtcose traits really exsit- I wonder how Lord DO I become her.

What ideas were new to you or showed you an area you need to pay more attention to?

I would have to agree on becoming a better housekeep. and to have more bible Reading time - with my Lord-

16

Searching for Treasure

Think of a gem or special piece of jewelry you own or know about. Why does it impress you, or what do you like about it? I am not much of jewel type of gal, but what (if I had to choose it would be a "diamond") They are so beautiful! How a real Diamond Sparkles is amazing to any eye sight — and the interesting part of this type of jewel, is that it needs to be worked on so that its the beauty comes to Thoes who can afford to own them!!

What gives it value?

The value that this jewel gives is that, it's one in a million, Every women wants to own one, and it can be a man's nightmare If he can't afford one, It is so beautiful that when a women puts this jewel on Weather on a finger, or on the neck it makes feel beautiful.

The How-To's of Beauty

1. *Grow in practical skills*—Note the references to home management, time management, and money management skills in Proverbs 31:10-31.

   Now think of yourself as God's precious jewel. How do you think these practical skills increase your value to those at home, church, work, and in your community?

   Home management—

   While being a Single women I believe, that I can better manasem my time by Learning housekeeping skills, Such As cooking, and Learning to eat ealther.

   Money management—

   It is always good to Learn how to monanne Credit Cards, banks cads, becaue we may Not know what Tomwarew holds - and Someae may Need yor help.

   Time management—

   We must Always include time fer our lordi famiry when ministres - All Shall fall Into placei If we have time fer our lordi IN Sauing this meaning bible Reading time

2. *Grow in emotional stability*—How or why does emotional stability increase your value to your husband, children, parents, friends, employer, and co-workers?

Emotional stability, Increases my value, in many ways, I feel that if I were to hae control of my emotions, I would hae a clear mind to help others around me.

Look up and list the character qualities encouraged in each of these passages. Also note what you can do to make each quality part of your daily life. Be specific.

Proverbs 14:30—"A heart at peace gives life, to the body, but envy rots the bones"

Give off the joy.

To be a peace with oneself, is truly a great witness to thoes who need peace in the lord

Proverbs 19:2b—"It is not good to have zeal without knowledge nor to be hasty and miss the way"

It must be known to accure knowledge in order to have the lord help you thrown decision maxg

Proverbs 19:11—"A mans wisdom gives him Patience, It is is glory to overlook an offense

If as women we could learn to be patient, how much better would it be to awent upon Geil

Proverbs 25:28—"Like a city whose walls are broken down, is a man who lacks self control

An Invitation to Beauty

What steps can you take to gain greater emotional stability? I need to Not allow things get to me. Not to cry der Evory little things that I don't like. I need to grow to be a strenger woman.

What steps can you take to sharpen your practical skills? For instance...

Books to read?
I belive IN this Area of my life I am growing. I want to become a better women IN the Lord.

Classes to take?
I feel that I need to Attain more women self help seminars, and learn to know what the Lord has for us.

Women who can mentor you in your practical skills?
Yes I do hae a frend who I belive IS a Great mentor IN my life.

Other activities?
MORE women fellowships!! IS A MUSt!

A Solid Rock
Her Loyalty

Read the chapter in *Beautiful in God's Eyes* titled "A Solid Rock—Her Loyalty." How did this chapter encourage you?

This chapter encourage me in many ways. For one I learned to have moe stability emotionally in my life. I realized that the women who loved their husbands learned to be stable in every area of there lives. They learned that if they give it all to the Lord that he will make them Beautiful in his Eyes

How did it challenge you?

The emotional stability aspect challenged me most, Because I tend to let things get to me! I am extremly sensitve I realize that at times it may show signs of weakness

What ideas were new to you or showed you an area you need to pay more attention to?

I feel that the area I need to grow most in is in how I deal with life emotionally. I need to learn that I should give Everything to the Lord, and NOT to Fret on the small things

The Language of Loyalty

Rest—What are the indications that your husband or someone else in your life "rests" in your support?

When they ask mae For Advice,
or they rely on me to heup
Them in Areas of there
lives. It's encourageing to knew
That People trust you!! They
Know I will aways be there
Fer them.

Encouragement—What have you done this week to be an encouragement to your husband? To others?

After bible study on Theresday I
went to visit a wonderful member
we say down and spoke about Things
That mean allot to both of us.
I belive by seeing her. I encarse
her by being there for her.

Trust in God—How do you respond to the thought that your husband and the people in your life should be able to trust you as they trust God?

I belive It's a wonderful feeling
that People who see the Lord
in your lae can trust you
with any area of there lives,
they know that God has done
a mighty Work, and may
also be a great testomey
of your lae for christ.

Checklist for Loyalty

Trustworthiness is the first character trait mentioned in Proverbs 31:10-31. Consider how trustworthy you are in the following areas. Note the areas where you are solid. Also note where you are improving...and where you need to improve.

Improving

Money (Proverbs 31:27)— Watches aer the household and does Not eat the bread of Idleness

No Chuldi'

Children (Proverbs 31:1-2)— Sawings of King Lemuel, from his mother. who taught him to find a virtas wife "O my son, o son of my womb, oh son of my vows

Improv

Home (Proverbs 31:13,27)— Watches aer the Afairs of her household, makes clothing Sales, clothed with streng and Dignito. Laghs as the days to come. Speaks with wisdom.

Im Solidy

Reputation (Proverbs 31:12,23)— Brings Gusel not horm, works with eager hand, brings Food from afar. Get's up while still Dans, buys a field, streng Arms, lamps Does not Go at, orpens her Arm to the bori

Solid

Fidelity (Proverbs 5:18)— "may yar fantain be blessed and may you rejoice in the wife of yar yath"

Improv

Emotions (Proverbs 14:30)— "A heart of Peace Gives life to the bones but enyy rots the bones.

Improve

Happiness (Psalm 37:4)—

Delight yourself in the Lord
and he will give you the
Desires of your heart *Ated*

Improve

Wisdom (Proverbs 19:14)—

Houses and wealth are inherited
from Parents, but a prudent
Wife is from the Lord

Conduct

Proverbs 11:16— A Kind hearted
women Gains respect, but ruthless
men gain only wealth

Proverbs 11:22— like a gold ring in
a pigs snout is a Beautiful
women who shows No
discreation

Proverbs 31:10— A wife of a noble
Character who can find?

Proverbs 31:25—

She Is clothed with
stength and dignity

Love (Proverbs 31:29)—

MAny women do
Noble things but you
Surpress them all

The How-To's of Beauty

1. *Take trust seriously*—What are you doing that indicates how seriously you are taking the responsibility of your husband's trust in you? Of others' trust in you?

When some IN trust's you IN a secret, Don't Judge them, or go and tell others, For this is untrctullres.

2. *Keep your word*—How would you rate yourself as one who keeps her appointments, and who does what she says? Why? Not very well, But I am learning to Not say yes on alot of Issues, or events, but to take them up with the Lord.

3. *Follow through on instructions*—How does your normal willingness and attitude rate when you are given instructions by someone else about how to do something? Why? Also Not very well, It takes time for me to actoally do something I must think about first—or I'll, will not want to do it.

4. *When in doubt, check it out!*—How willingly do you seek counsel from your husband? From an older woman? From others?

I would say alot, But I am not sure that I want to really hear it, Becase Its when I Shold do.

5. *Be accountable*—How does accountability nurture trust? To whom are you accountable?

I am accountable to God, to my family, friends, Accantabilty Natures trust becase, When you held accantable, for something what you say or do, others expect you, to do it, or say it

An Invitation to Beauty

❦

Read Genesis 3:1-6, the account of Eve's failure to be trustworthy and loyal. How did she fail her husband? (See also Genesis 2:17.) How did she fail God?

she failed her husband by Not speaking to him at what she shewed too first. she did not listen and Trust the lord commands for her life

Note here God's further comments on Eve's fall in...

2 Corinthians 11:3—

Just as eve was decieved by the servant's cunning your minds may some who be led astray from your sincere pure devtion to christ.

1 Timothy 2:14—

And Adam was not the one decieved. it was the women who was decieved and become a sinner.

What conclusions can you make regarding the importance of trust?

It is the atmost important thing to hae trust in the lord and and your family, who shews usell

Write out a prayer asking God to help you become more trustworthy.

help me lord to trust in you and those you hae sent my way Amen.

- 4 -

An Unfailing Prize
Her Contribution

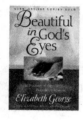 Read the chapter in *Beautiful in God's Eyes* titled "An Unfailing Prize—Her Contribution." How did this chapter encourage you?

How did it challenge you?

What ideas were new to you or showed you an area you need to pay more attention to?

The Spoils of War

What activities have you undertaken this past week in the "battle" to ensure that there is a "prize" and that there is financial security for you and your husband?

The "Warrior"

How do you see yourself as a warrior in the battle for your family finances or your personal finances?

The Beauty of God's Plan

Read through Proverbs 31:10-31 again, and jot down how the virtue of financial stewardship revealed in these verses is involved in each of these aspects that applies to your life:

God is honored and His causes are advanced—

Your husband is blessed—

Your children benefit—

Your home is built—

Your character grows—

A Personal Story

As you consider the powerful contribution you can make to your personal and family finances, briefly note the instructions these Scriptures offer to your own "personal story"...if applied. Also note one step in the right direction you can take right away.

Proverbs 10:2—

Proverbs 10:4—

Proverbs 13:11—

Proverbs 14:23—

Proverbs 21:6—

Proverbs 21:17—

Proverbs 27:23-24—

Proverbs 28:19 —

The How-To's of Beauty

List some goals you can make in each of these steps as you become a beautiful money manager—an unfailing prize.

1. Own the assignment—

2. Bone up on money management—

3. Talk it over with your husband—

4. Get set up for better money management—

An Invitation to Beauty

ↀ

You want to become a woman of virtue, character, godliness, and spiritual beauty. Realize your contribution in the financial area can be a thing of beauty. According to Proverbs 22:4, what other ultimate riches should you set your heart on? Write out at least three actions you can take to pursue—and obtain—such riches.

- 5 -

A Spring of Goodness
Her Mission

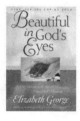

Read the chapter in *Beautiful in God's Eyes* titled "A Spring of Goodness—Her Mission." How did this chapter encourage you?

How did it challenge you?

What ideas were new to you or showed you an area you need to pay more attention to?

A Heart of Goodness

The presence of good—What steps are you taking to ensure the presence of good and goodness in your life?

The absence of evil—What steps are you taking to protect yourself against the temptations toward evil?

The influence of a lifetime—If you are married, write down your lifelong commitment to do your husband good. (It may have even been part of your marriage vows.) Once it is written, read it to your husband!

An Example of Goodness

How does the example of Lettie Cowman inspire you in your quest to do your husband—or others—good?

Do you have an inspiring example of beautiful feminine goodness from your own life acquaintances? Who is she, and what is her example to you?

The How-To's of Beauty

1. *Beware the enemies of goodness!*—Beginning with Eve, scan again the list of women in the Bible who failed to be springs of goodness for their husbands. What warnings do these women offer you as a woman and/or wife?

What effects have any of these heart issues had on your desire for goodness, and how did you deal with them?

A tendency to compare—

A growing root of bitterness—

A sagging spiritual condition—

2. *Follow God's plan*—What do these verses teach you as a Christian about following in Jesus' steps, about doing good to all people?

   Proverbs 3:27—

   Galatians 6:10—

   What perspective on God's challenging command to do good does Colossians 3:23 offer?

   How can this same truth help you do good in a difficult relationship right now?

Some ABCs of Goodness

Try your hand at completing the ABCs of goodness in your book. Or better yet, write your own alphabet of goodness—and then start living it out!

An Invitation to Beauty

⌒

How long is the Proverbs 31 woman to live out
Proverbs 31:12?

What changes could this perspective make in your
marriage? In your focus on doing good to others?

What will you do today to begin doing good "all the
days of your life"? Be specific. God wants you to be a
spring of goodness!

6

𝒜 Fountain of Joy
Her Heart

∽

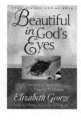

Read the chapter in *Beautiful in God's Eyes* titled "A Fountain of Joy—Her Heart." How did this chapter encourage you?

How did it challenge you?

What ideas were new to you or showed you an area you need to pay more attention to?

A Willing Worker

What key attitude toward work do these Scriptures stress?

Proverbs 31:13—

Ecclesiastes 9:10—

How would you evaluate your attitude toward the effort that is needed in your home and work place? What makes you say this?

What do you think will improve your attitude?

A Worker of Beauty

Why do you think your attitude is important…

To your Christianity?

To those at home and work?

To your homemaking?

To the atmosphere at home?

To God?

The How-To's of Beauty

What plans can you make to put each of these "attitude helpers" to work for you in your daily life? (Be sure to also look at your future tasks.) Jot down at least one step—something specific, something that can be measured—under each "attitude."

1. *Pray daily* (When and where?)—

2. *Recite Scripture* (What passage?)—

3. *Do your work as unto the Lord* (What does Colossians 3:23 say?)—

4. *Tackle your tasks* (Look up Colossians 3:17, record its message, and then evaluate the way you do your work.)

   Energetically—

   Creatively—

   Joyfully—

5. *Look for the benefits* (There must be something that can be gained by doing this task. What is it?)—

6. *Pause and rest* (Note the message of Matthew 11:28 and how it can give you rest...even in the midst of your labors.)—

7. *Watch what you eat* (Note the messages of 1 Corinthians 10:31 and Galatians 5:23. Then write down your action.)—

8. *Value each day* (How does Psalm 118:24 say you are to approach today...and every day?)—

An Invitation to Beauty

୬

What message does God have for you in the following verses about being a fountain of joy for your family and others?

Proverbs 15:15—

Proverbs 18:14—

Galatians 5:22—

What changes do you need to make in your attitude about your work in your home...and in life?

Ask God to fill your heart with His joy for your home, your family, your work, and the people in your life.

7

An Enterprising Spirit
Her Provision

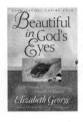

Read the chapter in *Beautiful in God's Eyes* titled "An Enterprising Spirit—Her Provision." How did this chapter encourage you?

How did it challenge you?

What ideas were new to you or showed you an area you need to pay more attention to?

A Spirit of Adventure

How does seeing your provision for your family members as an exciting and challenging adventure help give you the needed energy for God's assignment?

A Spirit of Mission

How does knowing that you are on a mission from God to provide for your family's needs motivate you?

A Spirit of Satisfaction

List some of the forms of satisfaction you receive as you think about what's best for others and then set about to provide it.

Are there areas where you are not satisfied? Identify them and write down some steps you can take to remedy this.

The How-To's of Beauty

1. *A heart of love*

   Pray—What should be your prayer toward your roles as a home manager, wife, mother, and family member?

   Make home your first priority—Married or not, has your home been a priority in your life? If not, what can you do to turn your attitude around, to turn your heart toward home?

   Spend time with other women—What steps can you take today toward spending time with another woman who makes her home a priority?

2. *A vision of loveliness*

   Surround yourself with beauty—What inexpensive ways can this be done in your home?

   Make your vision of loveliness a reality—What steps can you take in this area?

3. God's assignment to love

Start with the basics—List the basics that you and your family need.

Become a wise shopper—Now that you are aware of the basics, according to your book, what two attitudes do you need to have, and how can you become better at each?

—Focus on…

—Look for…

Search for the unusual—Where do you go to find the unusual? Share an example.

Consider bartering—What do you have or can make that could be used in this way?

Become "the resident artist"—What can you do to develop your artistic ability?

An Invitation to Beauty

❧

Take a minute to read Proverbs 9:1-6. As you press your hands and face against the window of God's Word, describe the scene in this wise woman's house— her food, her table, her home, her work, her goals, and the results.

What traits were key to her homemaking?

Now look at Proverbs 9:13-18. What do you see through the window of this woman's house—her food, her table, her home, her work, her goals, and the results?

Why was her homemaking so different from the scene described in Proverbs 9:1-6?

Describe what other people (especially your family members) see when they look through your window at your provision. How is your love evidenced in the basics such as the food you prepare and serve? The way you set the table? The way you've furnished your home? The personal touches of beauty you've added to the decor?

What impresses you about the provision described in 1 Kings 10:1-10?

What will you do to express your love as you—creatively and with touches of beauty—provide the basics for your family? For others? Be specific and star one step on your list that you will take today.

- 8 -

A Pattern for the Household
Her Discipline

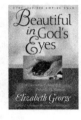

Read the chapter in *Beautiful in God's Eyes* titled "A Pattern for the Household—Her Discipline." How did this chapter encourage you?

How did it challenge you?

What ideas were new to you or showed you an area you need to pay more attention to?

Write out Proverbs 31:15 here, a verse that lists three essential disciplines that guarantee a beautifully run home:

Discipline #1: An Early Start

Look at the following verses and list some benefits of early rising.

Genesis 19:27—

Psalm 5:3—

Proverbs 16:3—

Proverbs 20:13—

Mark 1:35—

What steps will you take to develop this key and priceless discipline? Write out a brief plan for...

Tending the fire at home—

Tending the fire of your heart—

Tending the fires of the hearts of others—

Now, what would an ideal, yet reasonable, early hour be for your lifestyle?

Discipline #2: Food for the Family

List some benefits of meal preparation.

What warnings do these two verses offer about mealtime?

Proverbs 15:17—

Proverbs 17:1—

Plan your menus for a week. Make sure you have the ingredients and then provide "food to your household." They will rise up and call you blessed (Proverbs 31:28)!

Discipline #3: A Plan for the Day

What does God say about the discipline of planning in Proverbs 21:5?

List some benefits of planning out your day in advance.

Then make a plan for the rest of your day.

Tomorrow morning (hopefully early!) plan next week. And if you have children, don't forget to give a portion of your work to them.

A Pattern for Success

Getting up early each day will provide you with countless blessings. Describe how you have/would use each of these blessings in developing your own pattern of success.

Time alone—

Time with God—

Time to plan—

Time to get a jump on the day—

A Personal Story

You've read my story of how I benefit from getting up early. How are you doing in this area? Write out a few descriptive lines. (And take courage! If you have room for improvement, the next section will give you help.)

The How-To's of Beauty

Write down definite steps you can or will take in each discipline below:

1. Determine a bedtime—

2. Get to bed—

3. Say a prayer—

4. Get up!—

An Invitation to Beauty

How important do you believe your role in your home is? What commitment are you ready to make to your home, to your well-being, and to your family?

- 9 -

A Field of Dreams
Her Vision

Read the chapter in *Beautiful in God's Eyes* titled "A Field of Dreams—Her Vision." How did this chapter encourage you?

How did it challenge you?

What ideas were new to you or showed you an area you need to pay more attention to?

Triple Action

Look closely at the three steps for making a dream become reality.

Step 1: Consideration

What instruction does Proverbs 19:14 offer?

According to Proverbs 15:22 and Proverbs 12:15, what should your attitude toward counsel be?

List the people in your life you can—and will—turn to for wise counsel.

According to Proverbs 19:21, what should you pray for?

What role does waiting play in decision-making? (See Proverbs 21:5 and Proverbs 19:2.)

Step 2: Acquisition

What practical message regarding stewardship of your property do you find in...

Proverbs 14:1—

Proverbs 31:27—

Step 3: Renovation

Read through the story of Caleb's daughter Achsah in Joshua 15:13-19. What did she do to improve her property?

Why was she able to accomplish this?

Why do you think she made the requests she did?

The How-To's of Beauty

1. *Desire God's beauty*—Look again at the virtues under this area. Which ones would you like God to further work on in your life?

2. *Devote yourself to God's goals*—Look up the following verses in your Bible to discover some of God's goals for you...and your family.

    Proverbs 14:1—

    Proverbs 22:1—

    Proverbs 31:28—

3. *Your husband is paramount*—Remind yourself of what God says about a wife's relationship with her husband.

   Genesis 2:24 (this applies to the wife as well)—

   Ephesians 5:22—

   Ephesians 5:33b—

   Titus 2:4—

4. *Creativity abounds!*—What wild and wonderful thing have you been thinking about doing to your home (even on limited resources)?

5. *Dare to dream!*—Name one dream you have for yourself and your family for the future. Then note what you can do today to move toward making that dream a reality.

6. *Do the work!*—How badly do you want to see your dreams materialize? Enough to do the work that makes it happen? Please explain your answer.

   What "work" will it take to get your dream going? When are you going to start?

An Invitation to Beauty

In addition to the work you've already begun on your dreams, write out other "fields of dreams" you are entertaining and then pray about them. Ask God to show you what He wants you to pursue.

An Eager Attitude
Her Work

Read the chapter in *Beautiful in God's Eyes* titled "An Eager Attitude—Her Work." How did this chapter encourage you?

How did it challenge you?

What ideas were new to you or showed you an area you need to pay more attention to?

Preparation for Work

List the actions and preparations for work seen in the Proverbs 31 woman in Proverbs 31:17. Then note how they fit into this definition of a "virtuous" woman: "She is an army of virtues."

What do Proverbs 14:23a and Proverbs 14:23b say about your work?

How does Proverbs 14:1 motivate you to work even harder?

What do Proverbs 19:15 and 24 teach about the discipline of work?

How can the truth of Psalm 118:24 help you develop a beautiful attitude toward your work?

A Personal Formula for Work

How would you evaluate your attitude toward your work in your home using the following four qualities of the heart?

Commitment—

Willingness—

Motivation—

Discipline—

The How-To's of Beauty

1. *Embrace God's will for your life*—State here what you believe is God's will for your life. Then tell why you are or are not embracing it.

2. *Stay in God's Word*—Continuing to read and study the Bible will help you keep your resolve. What steps are you taking to be in God's Word on a daily basis?

3. *Develop a vision*—What is your vision for yourself and your family? Name several dreams you have for yourself, your home, and your family.

4. *Tap into the why*—Again, state the "why" of your vision for yourself and your family.

5. *Pray for an eager attitude*—Write out a one or two sentence prayer for an eager attitude toward your "home work." Try to incorporate one of the scriptures from this chapter or book into your prayer.

6. *Create a schedule*—What is your schedule for tomorrow? Once it's made, make one for the rest of the week.

7. *Develop a routine*—List below the activities and the times that you and your family do—or should do—certain things every day. (See your book for some samples.) Then place them on your daily schedule.

8. *Read books on time management*—What time management book have you chosen? If you haven't, ask someone for advice on a good book to read in this area.

9. *Tackle the worst first*—What is the worst thing that you will face tomorrow? Now that you've named it, slot in a time on your schedule tomorrow for working on it.

10. *Play music*—When you start your work, put on some lively music that will get your blood flowing...and then get started! What music will you play?

11. *See how quickly you can work*—Work, any work, will consume all the time you give it. So pick one project. Next, get out the kitchen timer and set it for five minutes. Work as hard as you can and as fast as you can. How far did you get? What progress was made? Set the timer for another five minutes, and see if you can work even faster.

	Project	**Results**
Round 1:		
Round 2:		

As you do your work, remember this principle:

"Work expands to fill the time allotted to it."

An Invitation to Beauty

∽

12. *Consider yourself*—So often we are our own worst enemy when it comes to getting things done on time and in an efficient manner. How often are you guilty of putting off a project because it seems so large or too big to tackle? Describe one instance.

Would you or others say you are a procrastinator? If so, what first step can you take to break this habit?

I invite you to talk to someone you know who excels at time management and get some tips… and encouragement. Also, sometime this week, borrow, buy, or check out from the library a book on time management. And above all, don't wait! Do it now!

- 11 -

A Taste of Success
Her Confidence

Read the chapter in *Beautiful in God's Eyes* titled "A Taste of Success—Her Confidence." How did this chapter encourage you?

How did it challenge you?

What ideas were new to you or showed you an area you need to pay more attention to?

Excellence in All Things

Read Proverbs 31:18 and Psalm 34:8. In what areas of your home would you or your family consider you to be doing an excellent job?

Is there a particular area that needs improvement?

Review the following points in your book and note what you can do to excel still more in these areas.

Excellent taste—

Excellent goods—

Excellent results—

Excellent pursuit—

A Stimulus to Excellence

What reasons for confidence do you find in...

Ecclesiastes 9:10—

Philippians 1:6—

Philippians 3:13-14—

Philippians 4:13—

Write out a prayer or a commitment based on Proverbs 16:3.

The How-To's of Beauty

1. *Listen to others*—Of the many things you do, what are other people saying is "good"?

2. *Move forward*—Have you tried something new lately and failed? What will it take to get you moving forward again?

3. *Develop your skills*—What skills are needed for an area of interest that might also become an area for producing a product for sale or use by your family?

4. *Redeem your time*—What activities have you eliminated from your life and schedule so that you can redeem some time? What activities can go?

5. *Take risks*—What new thing can you attempt? What's the worst thing that could happen if you fail?

6. *Do your best*—Read Ecclesiastes 9:10a. What does God desire of you?

7. *Do your projects unto the Lord*—Read Proverbs 16:3 and Colossians 3:23. What do these verses say about the focus of your efforts?

8. *Manage for profit*—How would you rate your home-managing skills? What can you do to improve in becoming a better steward of your resources?

9. *Become convinced*—What talents and abilities do you have that can be used to further your family's comfort, both physically and financially? Explain your answer.

10. *Family first*—Above all, what should be the motives behind all you do with your talents and abilities?

An Invitation to Beauty

و~

Look again at this chapter's "An Invitation to Beauty." What efforts have you made so far concerning the reminders mentioned there?

What are the results?

How high is your confidence in God and His plan for your life?

Spend time praying for yourself and for your family. Ask God to give you fresh ideas about how to love and serve. (Make any notes here.) Also ask Him to energize and fuel your creative desires and efforts.

- 12 -

A Little Night Work
Her Diligence

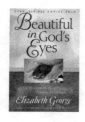

Read the chapter in *Beautiful in God's Eyes* titled "A Little Night Work—Her Diligence." How did this chapter encourage you?

How did it challenge you?

What ideas were new to you or showed you an area you need to pay more attention to?

Behind the Scenes

What tedious, unexciting, mundane chores do you usually fail to get around to doing—day or night?

What is your attitude about these "no-brainers"?

How has reading this chapter helped to change your attitude?

The How-To's of Beauty

1. *Evaluate your evenings*—Read Proverbs 31:18 and 19. What does God's beautiful woman do in the evening?

   What do you generally do in the evening?

2. *Plan your evenings*—Create a P.M. list of projects you can do in the evening.

   —
   —
   —
   —
   —

   What motivation for evening projects do you find in Proverbs 10:4? Can you think of other motivating scriptures?

3. *Prepare for your evenings*—What project can you work on tonight?

   What can you lay out, get ready, set up?

4. *Use your evenings!*—Look again at Proverbs 14:23. What encouragement for putting your plan into action and continuing to keep moving do you find in these words of wisdom?

5. *Use your mind in the evenings*—Jot down how you usually spend your evenings.

   Now write down at least three ways you can improve or begin to use your mind during these times.

   —

   —

   —

   How important is the proper use of your mind according to Proverbs 23:7 and Philippians 4:8?

An Invitation to Beauty

～

Evaluate your evenings in light of what you are learning in Proverbs 31:10-31. What one thing can you do to make your evenings more productive?

Just for this week, make a real effort to use your evenings constructively. After you see the benefits to you, your family, and others (and you will), repeat the process for another week—and continue for life!

Ask God to guide your heart and hands toward greater diligence in the evening. May the blessings be so evident that you make "a little night work" a habit!

A Helping Hand
Her Mercy

 Read the chapter in *Beautiful in God's Eyes* titled "A Helping Hand—Her Mercy." How did this chapter encourage you?

How did it challenge you?

What ideas were new to you or showed you an area you need to pay more attention to?

Her Hand

Look again at Proverbs 31:20. What are the activities God's beautiful woman is involved in here?

Her Hands

Read Proverbs 3:27 and then make a list of some of the good deeds you could do—deeds that are in the power of your hand to do, but deeds you could also choose not to do.

Her Heart

Note the teachings about a merciful heart found in the following scriptures:

Deuteronomy 15:7-8—

Proverbs 11:25—

Proverbs 19:17—

Proverbs 22:9—

Micah 6:8—

Her Heeding of God's Word

Looking at the verses under "Her Heart" on page 82, what conclusions can you draw about a giving spirit?

What are the evidences of your giving spirit?

What changes can or must you make?

Her Sisters of Mercy

Choose one of the following women, and briefly describe her acts of mercy. (As a bonus, do the same for all of these women!)

Abigail (1 Samuel 25)

The widow of Zarephath (1 Kings 17)

The Shunamite woman (2 Kings 4)

Women who ministered to Jesus (Luke 8:1-3)

Dorcas (Acts 9)

The How-To's of Beauty

1. *Begin at home*—What acts of mercy do your family and others see you perform? How can you involve them in these acts?

2. *Give regularly to your home church*—If you have children, what are you doing to teach them the importance of giving to God's work through your church?

3. *Keep your ear to the ground*—How can you do a better job of noticing the needs of others?

4. *Support a worthy organization or person*—What mission organization or missionary can you or your family take on as a giving project?

5. *Pray about a personal project*—Have you started praying? If not, begin today.

6. *Err on the side of generosity*—Read 2 Corinthians 9:6-10. What do these verses teach you about generosity?

An Invitation to Beauty

❧

7. *Live out love*—Read 1 Corinthians 13 and write out a brief evaluation of how well you live out love.

Spend time in prayer asking God to grow your love and show you more ways to live it out. (Make note here.)

My Prayer of Commitment
Lord of all beauty and grace,
help me to remember to improve or change
this one thing in my life:

- 14 -

A Double Blessing
Her Preparation

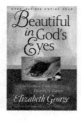

Read the chapter in *Beautiful in God's Eyes* titled "A Double Blessing—Her Preparation." How did this chapter encourage you?

How did it challenge you?

What ideas were new to you or showed you an area you need to pay more attention to?

Looking to the Future

Look again at Proverbs 31:21. What is said of the Proverbs 31 woman?

What is said of her household?

What plans are you making for your future well-being and that of your family?

"Extended Care" Living

As you think about your family, who are the people your care should be extended to?

How can you make sure this happens?

Clothes Fit for a King

Look again at the story of the Queen of Sheba (1 Kings 10:1-10). What impressed her about King Solomon's household?

What impresses you?

What improvements can you make after this glimpse of organized beauty?

Read Proverbs 21:5. What evidence in 1 Kings 10 do you see that King Solomon lived according to this wisdom?

The How-To's of Beauty

Take a few minutes to read this section in your book again.
Then prepare a to-do list with several items for each area of
concern. Be as specific as possible.

1. Determine future needs—

2. Prepare for emergencies—

3. Care for the clothing—

4. Consider quality—

5. Consider comfort—

6. Consider beauty—

An Invitation to Beauty

What specifically do you need to do to incorporate both advance preparation and attention to beauty into your homemaking efforts?

In Exodus 35:25, 26, and 29, God gives some instructions about building the tabernacle for worship. What do these verses suggest about how important creative beauty is to God?

What is God's message to your heart...and home?

- 15 -
A Tapestry of Beauty
Her Handiwork

cᘓ

 Read the chapter in *Beautiful in God's Eyes* titled "A Tapestry of Beauty—Her Handiwork." How did this chapter encourage you?

How did it challenge you?

What ideas were new to you or showed you an area you need to pay more attention to?

House Beautiful

Read Proverbs 31:22 to see what else God's beautiful woman does in her home. What preparation and touches of beauty do you read about here?

Beauty Check

Take a look around your own home to see if you are weaving a tapestry of beauty.

Check #1: Pretend you're a visitor—What do you see? What would a guest see? What are the eyesores?

Check #2: Plan several home improvements—What can be done for the least outlay of money?

Check #3: Pass it by your husband—Sometimes our financial condition requires that we wait before launching into home improvements. What encouragement for waiting does Proverbs 19:2b offer?

How can the message of Philippians 4:11-12 and 1 Timothy 6:6-8 help you when you must wait?

Check #4: Put in some overtime—Those projects that can be done now need to be scheduled. When can you start? Tonight? Next Saturday? Write it down on your calendar and get started!

A Touch of Class

Look back at Exodus 35:25-29. What details added beauty to the scene?

What do the following passages reveal about God's standards of beauty?

1 Timothy 2:9-10—

1 Peter 3:3-4—

Titus 2:5—

A Touch of Taste

How did each of these elements contribute to the Proverbs 31 woman's attention to beauty and creativity?

Position—

Practice—

Professional status—

Praiseworthy character—

The How-To's of Beauty

Consider what God is saying to you about your own personal wardrobe.

1. *Your care*—What message are you sending to others in the way you care for your appearance and your family's clothing?

2. *Your reflection*—What sort of reflection are you giving to others by the way you—and your family—dress?

3. *Your standards*—Review these verses and jot down any additional thoughts about what God says His standards are for the "clothing of your heart."

   1 Timothy 2:9—

   Titus 2:5—

   1 Peter 3:3-4—

An Invitation to Beauty

∽

According to Psalm 19:1, what evidence do we see of God's handiwork?

According to Psalm 139:14-16, what evidence do you see of God's handiwork in you?

Bow your heart and your head and thank God that you are created in His image (Genesis 1:27) and possess a measure of His beauty and creativity.

- 16 -

A Man of Influence
Her Husband

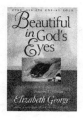 Read the chapter in *Beautiful in God's Eyes* titled "A Man of Influence—Her Husband." How did this chapter encourage you?

How did it challenge you?

What ideas were new to you or showed you an area you need to pay more attention to?

Marriage to a Man of Influence

How is the husband of the Proverbs 31 woman described in verse 23?

What did you learn about this description?

Now write your own brief description of this husband.

Behind Every Good Man

After reviewing Proverbs 31:23, read the passages listed below that set forth God's design for marriage. Make personal notes as you go.

Genesis 2:18—

Genesis 3:16—

Ephesians 5:22-24,33—

Colossians 3:18—

Titus 2:3-5—

1 Peter 3:1-6—

A Woman of Influence

What exhortations does a married woman find in these verses for enhancing her ministry to her husband (or to anyone else)?

Proverbs 3:27—

Proverbs 12:25—

Look in your Bible at the following scriptures and what they teach about ministering to your husband and to others. Then complete the prayer below, noting the single most important thing you can do to better minister to others, beginning at home.

Proverbs 31:12—the practice of doing good

Proverbs 31:15—meal preparation

Proverbs 31:15—orderly household management

Proverbs 31:21—the provision of clothing

Proverbs 31:26—wise counsel and kind speech

Proverbs 31:27—watch-care of the people and the place of home

Lord, with Your help, today I will begin to…

The How-To's of Beauty

If you are married, what "little thing" can you do in each of the following areas to duplicate the beautiful heart of the Proverbs 31 wife? If you are not married, look for God's instruction about ministering positively to others.

1. Praise him—

2. Encourage him—

3. Take care of your marriage—

4. Take care of your family—

5. Take care of your home—

6. Take care of your finances—

7. Let him go—

8. Support his dreams—

9. Realize that your behavior is a reflection on him…
   and Him!—

An Invitation to Beauty

Concentrate today on speaking a word of praise and encouragement to your husband and/or to others. That's the important first step toward making this ministry a daily habit! Then note here what you did and any results.

- 17 -

A Creative Professional
Her Industry

∽

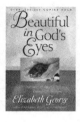 Read the chapter in *Beautiful in God's Eyes* titled "A Creative Professional—Her Industry." How did this chapter encourage you?

How did it challenge you?

What ideas were new to you or showed you an area you need to pay more attention to?

The Birth of a Business

Read Proverbs 31:24 again. What is God's beautiful woman doing here?

Read through Proverbs 31:10-31 and note here the references (or implied references) to weaving.

What seems to have been this woman's "something personal"?

The Expression of Creativity

What are your expressions of creativity?

What can you do to further develop these creative skills?

The Enrichment of Estate

Even though you may not have a "cottage industry," you still run a very significant "business" as you see to your life, your home, and your family life. What are some activities you are presently doing to further your "home estate" (like clipping coupons, watching for sales or bargains or closeouts, keeping better records of expenses, knowing your daily bank balance, etc.)?

What are some additional activities you can initiate?

A Personal Story

I shared a little about how my "something personal" became "something professional." Have you or someone you know done something similar? Briefly share about it here.

If you have turned something into a profession (however humble), what advice could you give to others?

If you know someone who did this, be sure to ask them for advice on how she made it happen.

How do these two elements fit into your plan for creative growth and development?

Your family is first—

Give it time—

The How-To's of Beauty

What/how can each of the following criteria for creativity contribute to the development of your skills?

1. Alertness—

2. Planning—

3. Initiative—

4. Hard work—

An Invitation to Beauty

❧

What do you love to do? What "something personal" has the potential of becoming "something professional"?

What three action steps can you take this week to move forward in your "something personal"?

- 18 -

A Wardrobe of Virtues
Her Clothing

 Read the chapter in *Beautiful in God's Eyes* titled "A Wardrobe of Virtues—Her Clothing." How did this chapter encourage you?

How did it challenge you?

What ideas were new to you or showed you an area you need to pay more attention to?

The Clothing of Character

Read Proverbs 31:25. What do you find most striking in this verse?

Look up the words "strength" and "dignity" and "honor" in a dictionary and note their definitions.

Strength—

Dignity—

Honor—

Now write a definition of each in your own words.

Strength—

Dignity—

Honor—

Joy for a Lifetime

Why do you think God's beautiful woman will rejoice in the future?

What do you think makes this rejoicing possible?

The How-To's of Beauty

Create a long-range plan for strengthening each of these aspects of your life:

1. Your spiritual life—

2. Your family life—

3. Your financial life—

4. Your physical life—

5. Your mental life—

6. Your social life—

7. Your professional life—

An Invitation to Beauty

◦◦

What two or three things can you do today to improve in several of these seven aspects of your life? When you are finished creating a list, offer up a prayer to God for His help...and then set about to enhance your "wardrobe of virtues."

- 19 -

A Law of Kindness
Her Words

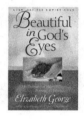

Read the chapter in *Beautiful in God's Eyes* titled "A Law of Kindness—Her Words." How did this chapter encourage you?

How did it challenge you?

What ideas were new to you or showed you an area you need to pay more attention to?

A Fountain of Life

Note the two elements of beautiful speech in Proverbs 31:26.

Wise in Speech

Think for a moment about the quality and content of your speech. Check those below where you are doing well—or better—and thank God.

___Wise and kind speech

___Sweet speech

___Thinking before you speak

___Persuasive speech

___Waiting before you speak

___Not speaking too often

Now star the ones you want or need to improve.

How will you go about making improvements?

Kind in Heart
Read Ephesians 4:29. How does this verse fulfill the law of kindness?

How does it ensure godly content?

Absence of Malice
Read James 3:1-12. Describe the potential harm that words can do.

Listening to God's Beautiful Women
Choose either Hannah or Abigail as a model of wise and kind speech and explain what she teaches about the proper use of "sweet speech." (Or, as a bonus, choose both women!)

Hannah (1 Samuel 1:1-7)—

Abigail (1 Samuel 25)—

The How-To's of Beautiful Speech

1. *Establish two guidelines*—List again the two guidelines for your speech from Proverbs 31:26.

   ___

   ___

   What can you do to remember each of these two restraints for your speech? Be creative!

   ___

   ___

2. *Think before you speak*—How does James 1:19 reinforce this principle?

3. *Learn to wait*—What happened the last time you failed to follow the principle of "doing nothing or saying nothing"?

What can you do in the following areas to further move toward developing a pattern of speech that is both wise and kind?

  4. *Add sweetness to your speech—*

  5. *Add persuasiveness to your speech—*

  6. *Err on the side of less—*

An Invitation to Beauty

The way we speak becomes a habit, and habits can be changed. What can you do today to improve the areas where you are weak?

Which one(s) will you institute right away...and how?

(P.S.: Don't forget to ask God for His divine help!)

- 20 -

A Watchful Eye
Her Management

∽

Read the chapter in *Beautiful in God's Eyes* titled "A Watchful Eye—Her Management." How did this chapter encourage you?

How did it challenge you?

What ideas were new to you or showed you an area you need to pay more attention to?

Keeping Watch Over Her Flock

Write out Proverbs 31:27 and memorize it.

What aspect(s) of your homemaking needs your loving watch-care?

And most important, who in your household needs your watch-care?

In what ways does and would your household benefit from your diligent watching? (A quick look at recent weeks will help you answer this question.)

What potential problems can your oversight prevent?

Keeping Watch Over Herself

What do the following proverbs teach about eating "the bread of idleness" and its results?

Proverbs 6:9-11—

Proverbs 10:4-5—

Proverbs 12:24—

Proverbs 19:15—

Proverbs 20:4—

Proverbs 26:14—

What is the main message to your heart...and your management?

The How-To's of Beauty

First the people—What steps must you take to better watch over the people in your home?

Then the place—What steps must you take to better watch over your physical home?

An Invitation to Beauty

Proverbs 31:27 is a two-part description, half spoken in the positive and half in the negative. Plan some specific steps you will take toward strengthening the positive (watching over your household).

Now plan some specific steps you will take toward eliminating the negative (eating the bread of idleness).

Be sure to commit your plan to the Lord and allow Him to establish it (Proverbs 16:3).

A Cup of Blessing
Her Family

Read the chapter in *Beautiful in God's Eyes* titled "A Cup of Blessing—Her Family." How did this chapter encourage you?

How did it challenge you?

What ideas were new to you or showed you an area you need to pay more attention to?

A Blessed Mother

Look again at Proverbs 31:28. What scene is pictured here, and who is present?

Essential #1: A Mother Cares

If you are a mother, what gift of care can you give to your children today in each area below? And tomorrow? Or, if you have younger siblings or nieces and nephews, what can you do for them in answer to the questions in this lesson? Remember, it's all about your heart!

...the gift of the basics—

Today?

Tomorrow?

...the gift of time—

Today?

Tomorrow?

...the gift of long-distance love—

Today?

Tomorrow?

Essential #2: A Mother Focuses

What has been the focus of your mothering? Has it been on spiritual things or on the things of this world? Please explain.

What changes do you need to make in your focus?

Essential #3: A Mother Plans

...the presence of the Lord—Describe how you are presently filling your heart with God's Word.

...pass on faith in Jesus Christ—Describe what you are presently doing daily to instill God's truth into your children's hearts.

What is your weekly pattern for church attendance?

...a pleasant atmosphere in the home—How is your home looking? Looking back at these past weeks of studying this book and applying the message of Proverbs 31 to your heart and home, what new-and-improved memories do you think your family now has?

How has this changed from the past?

...progressing relationships—How have you improved in the practice of planning times with your children? Share an example.

...persistence—Based on age and development, where are each of your children on the 100-yard playing field?

What will you do to see that (Lord willing!) your children "go the distance"?

What steps must you take to be more persistent in your parenting?

Essential #4: A Mother Works

Describe the work habits of the mother who is teaching her son the wisdom of Proverbs 31.

What changes do you need to make in your life?

But What if...?

You and I are not to focus on outcomes. Outcomes are up to God. But we are to fulfill our roles and responsibilities. What instructions do the following Scriptures give for mothers?

Titus 2:4—

Proverbs 1:8—

Proverbs 22:6—

Proverbs 29:17—

Proverbs 31:27—

An Invitation to Beauty

∽

After reading about Dr. Bill Bright's mother, how does her life and devotion motivate you and your mothering efforts? Also, if you think of other godly mothers, share from their examples as well.

- 22 -

A Crowning Chorus
Her Praise

Read the chapter in *Beautiful in God's Eyes* titled "A Crowning Chorus—Her Praise." How did this chapter encourage you?

How did it challenge you?

What ideas were new to you or showed you an area you need to pay more attention to?

An Excellent Wife

Read Proverbs 31:28 and 29 again. What is your first response or thought concerning the husband's praise?

An Army of Virtuous Women

"Many daughters have done well," says the husband of God's beautiful woman, a man who sat in the gates and observed the people of his region. Can you think of some of the "many" women in the Bible who did well? List them here.

Exactly what did they do?

What specific things will you do to follow in their footsteps?

The Best of All!

Could others or your husband say "you excel them all" about your character and the fulfillment of your roles in the home and as a wife, mother, and contributor to the community? Why or why not?

Can you think of one or two improvements that you can make?

A Kaleidoscope of Virtues

Read Proverbs 31:10-31 again, noting the dominant virtues in this woman and how other people (and the husband of the Proverbs 31 woman) benefited from each.

A Beautiful Crown

Read again Proverbs 12:4. If you are married, how would you evaluate and describe yourself as the "crown" your husband wears? What could you do to make yourself a "brighter ornament" for your husband?

But What if...?

How did each of these women exhibit beauty in the midst of a difficult marriage?

Hannah—

Abigail—

Esther—

An Invitation to Beauty

Look at the questions being asked of you under this section. Prayerfully answer as many as you can, asking God to strengthen your virtues...

As a woman—

As a homemaker—

As a mother—

As a wife—

- 23 -

A Spirit of Reverence
Her Faith

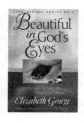 Read the chapter in *Beautiful in God's Eyes* titled "A Spirit of Reverence—Her Faith." How did this chapter encourage you?

How did it challenge you?

What ideas were new to you or showed you an area you need to pay more attention to?

The Twin Vanities of Charm and Beauty

Read Proverbs 31:30 again. Jot down the warning and the exhortation.

Look up the words "charm" and "favor" and "beauty" in a dictionary. Then write a definition of each in your own words.

—

—

—

Where do you think most women place their focus, and why?

Where do you generally place *your* focus? What contributes to this?

Do any changes need to be made? If so, what specific changes will you make?

A Love for the Lord

How would you explain "the fear of the Lord" to someone else?

What insights do these Proverbs give about "the fear of the Lord"?

Proverbs 1:7—

Proverbs 8:13—

Proverbs 9:10—

Proverbs 15:33—

Proverbs 22:4—

Proverbs 31:30—

What misuse of charm is described in the following verses?

Proverbs 21:6—

Proverbs 7:21—

Proverbs 5:3—

The How-To's of Beauty

1. *More love to Thee, O Christ*—According to your book, what is the key to being beautiful in God's eyes?

   Now I ask you, what is *your* beauty based on?

   How does time with the Lord enhance your beauty?

2. *Schedule time with the Lord*—What will you do to spend more time with God, basking in the beauty of His holiness (Psalm 27:4)? List four improvements.

3. *Embrace God's plan*—Review again God's plan for your life. Which area or areas need greater attention, and why?

What do you plan to do about these areas?

4. *Do your best*—Do you agree or disagree that your physical condition increases or decreases your ability to care for your family and others? Why?

How are you doing at balancing physical fitness and bringing honor to your family? List any changes that must be made.

An Invitation to Beauty

Read the prayer in this section in your book. Can you confidently say that Jesus Christ is your personal Savior? Why or why not?

- 24 -

The Harvest of a Lifetime
Her Reward

∼

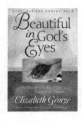 Read the chapter in *Beautiful in God's Eyes* titled "The Harvest of a Lifetime—Her Reward." How did this chapter encourage you?

How did it challenge you?

What ideas were new to you or showed you an area you need to pay more attention to?

The Fruit of Her Hands

Keep in mind as you work this lesson that we are reviewing God's beautiful woman's character and Proverbs 31:10-31. Read God's final word about beauty in Proverbs 31:31 and note the two commands.

—

—

What impresses you most about this tribute or epitaph?

—

Now take pen in hand and praise God's beautiful and excellent woman. What do you find praiseworthy in her?

What is your favorite trait about her? Why?

Praise in the Gates

Think about all that God's beautiful woman has accomplished. What impresses you most about her? About her accomplishments?

God's beautiful woman deserves all the praise we or those at "the gate" can give her. Why? Because of her hard work and the motivation behind her work! What message do the following Proverbs offer your heart—and your hands— about the beauty and value of hard work?

Proverbs 14:23—

Proverbs 27:18—

Proverbs 28:19—

Proverbs 31:13—

Proverbs 31:31—

An Invitation to Beauty

❧

What has your study of the woman who is beautiful in God's eyes shown you about God's will for your life? Take a few minutes to express your thoughts and convictions in writing. This should be a life-changing exercise, and you'll want to keep your written words and refer to them often. End this study by offering up a heartfelt prayer of praise to God and a commitment to Him and His beautiful ways.

Leading a Bible Study Discussion Group

~

What a privilege it is to lead a Bible study! And what joy and excitement await you as you delve into the Word of God and help others to discover its life-changing truths. If God has called you to lead a Bible study group, I know you'll be spending much time in prayer and planning and giving much thought to being an effective leader. I also know that taking the time to read through the following tips will help you to navigate the challenges of leading a Bible study discussion group and to enjoy the effort and opportunity.

The Leader's Roles

As a Bible study group leader, you'll find your role changing back and forth from *leader* to *cheerleader* to *lover* to *referee* during the course of a session.

Since you're the leader, group members will look to you to be the *leader* who guides them through the material. So be well prepared. In fact, be over-prepared so that you know the material better than any group member does. Start your study early in the week and let its message simmer all week long. (You might even work several lessons ahead so that you have in mind the big picture and the overall direction of the study.) Be ready to share some additional gems that your group members wouldn't have discovered on their own. That extra insight from your study time—or that comment from a wise Bible teacher or scholar, that clever saying, that keen observation from another believer, and even an appropriate joke—adds an element of fun and keeps Bible study from becoming routine, monotonous, and dry.

Next, be ready to be the group's *cheerleader*. Your energy and enthusiasm for the task at hand can be contagious. It can also stimulate people to get more involved in their personal study as well as in the group discussion.

Third, be the *lover*, the one who shows a genuine concern for the members of the group. You're the one who will establish the atmosphere of the group. If you laugh and have fun, the group members will laugh and have fun. If you hug, they will hug. If you care, they will care. If you share, they will share. If you love, they will love. So pray every day to love the women God has placed in your group. Ask Him to show you how to love them with His love.

Finally, as the leader, you'll need to be the *referee* on occasion. That means making sure everyone has an equal opportunity to speak. That's easier to do when you operate under the assumption that every member of the group has something worthwhile to contribute. So, trusting that the Lord has taught each person during the week, act on that assumption.

Leader, cheerleader, lover, and referee—these four roles of the leader may make the task seem overwhelming. But that's not bad if it keeps you on your knees praying for your group.

A Good Start

Beginning on time, greeting people warmly, and opening in prayer gets the study off to a good start. Know what you want to have happen during your time together and make sure those things get done. That kind of order means comfort for those involved.

Establish a format and let the group members know what that format is. People appreciate being in a Bible study that focuses on the Bible. So keep the discussion on the topic and move the group through the questions. Tangents are often hard to avoid—and even harder to rein in. So be sure to focus on the answers to questions about the specific passage at hand. After all, the purpose of the group is Bible study!

Finally, as someone has accurately observed, "Personal growth is one of the by-products of any effective small group. This growth is achieved when people are recognized and accepted by others. The more friendliness, mutual trust, respect, and warmth exhibited, the more likely it is that the member will find pleasure in the group, and, too, the more likely she will work hard toward the accomplishment of the group's goals. The effective leader will strive to reinforce desirable traits" (source unknown).

A Dozen Helpful Tips

Here is a list of helpful suggestions for leading a Bible study discussion group:

1. Arrive early, ready to focus fully on others and give of yourself. If you have to do any last-minute preparation, review, re-grouping, or praying, do it in the car. Don't dash in, breathless, harried, late, still tweaking your plans.

2. Check out your meeting place in advance. Do you have everything you need—tables, enough chairs, a whiteboard, hymnals if you plan to sing, coffee, etc.?

3. Greet each person warmly by name as she arrives. After all, you've been praying for these women all week long, so let each VIP know that you're glad she's arrived.

4. Use name tags for at least the first two or three weeks.

5. Start on time no matter what—even if only one person is there!

6. Develop a pleasant but firm opening statement. You might say, "This lesson was great! Let's get started so we can enjoy all of it!" or "Let's pray before we begin our lesson."

7. Read the questions, but don't hesitate to reword them on occasion. Rather than reading an entire paragraph of instructions, for instance, you might say, "Question 1 asks us to list some ways that Christ displayed humility. Lisa, please share one way Christ displayed humility."

8. Summarize or paraphrase the answers given. Doing so will keep the discussion focused on the topic, eliminate digressions, help avoid or clear up any misunderstandings of the text, and keep each group member aware of what the others are saying.

9. Keep moving and don't add any of your own questions to the discussion time. It's important to get through the study guide questions. So if a cut-and-dried answer is called for, you don't need to comment with anything other than a "thank you." But when the question asks for an opinion or an application (for instance, "How can this truth help us in our marriages?" or "How do *you* find time for your quiet time?"), let all who want to contribute do so.

10. Affirm each person who contributes, especially if the contribution was very personal, painful to share, or a quiet person's rare statement. Acknowledge everyone who shares as a hero by saying something like "Thank you for sharing that insight from your own life" or "We certainly appreciate what God has taught you. Thank you for letting us in on it."

11. Watch your watch, put a clock right in front of you, or consider using a timer. Pace the discussion so that you meet your cut-off time, especially if you want time to pray. Stop at the designated time even if you haven't finished the lesson. Remember that everyone has worked through the study once. You are simply going over it again.

12. End on time. You can only make friends with your group members by ending on time or even a little early! Besides, members of your group have the next item on their agenda to attend to—picking up children from the nursery or babysitter or school, heading home to tend to matters there, running errands, getting to bed, or spending some time with their husbands. So let them out on time!

Five Common Problems

In any group, you can anticipate certain problems. Here are some common ones that can arise, along with helpful solutions:

1. *The incomplete lesson*—Right from the start, establish the policy that if someone has not done the lesson, it is best for her not to answer the questions. But do try to include her responses to questions that ask for opinions or experiences. Everyone can share some thoughts in reply to a question like "Reflect on what you know about both athletic and spiritual training, and then share what you consider to be the essential elements of training oneself in godliness."

2. *The gossip*—The Bible clearly states that gossiping is wrong, so you don't want to allow it in your group. Set a high and strict standard by saying, "I am not comfortable with this conversation," or "We [not *you*] are gossiping, ladies. Let's move on."

3. *The talkative member*—Here are three scenarios and some possible solutions for each.

   a. The problem talker may be talking because she has done her homework and is excited about something she has to share. She may also know more about the subject than the others and, if you cut her off, the rest of the group may suffer.

   SOLUTION: Respond with a comment like, "Sarah, you are making very valuable contributions. Let's see if we can get some reactions from the others," or "I know Sarah can answer this. She's really done her homework. How about some of the rest of you?"

   b. The talkative member may be talking because she has *not* done her homework and wants to contribute, but she has no boundaries.

   SOLUTION: Establish at the first meeting that those who have not done the lesson do not contribute except on opinion or application questions. You may need to repeat this guideline at the beginning of each session.

   c. The talkative member may want to be heard whether or not she has anything worthwhile to contribute.

   SOLUTION: After subtle reminders, be more direct, saying, "Betty, I know you would like to share your ideas, but let's give others a chance. I'll call on you later."

4. *The quiet member*—Here are two scenarios and possible solutions.

   a. The quiet member wants the floor but somehow can't get the chance to share.

SOLUTION: Clear the path for the quiet member by first watching for clues that she wants to speak (moving to the edge of her seat, looking as if she wants to speak, perhaps even starting to say something) and then saying, "Just a second. I think Chris wants to say something." Then, of course, make her a hero!

b. The quiet member simply doesn't want the floor.

SOLUTION: "Chris, what answer do you have on question 2?" or "Chris, what do you think about...?" Usually after a shy person has contributed a few times, she will become more confident and more ready to share. Your role is to provide an opportunity where there is *no* risk of a wrong answer. But occasionally a group member will tell you that she would rather not be called on. Honor her request, but from time to time ask her privately if she feels ready to contribute to the group discussions.

In fact, give all your group members the right to pass. During your first meeting, explain that any time a group member does not care to share an answer, she may simply say, "I pass." You'll want to repeat this policy at the beginning of every group session.

5. *The wrong answer*—Never tell a group member that she has given a wrong answer, but at the same time never let a wrong answer go by.

SOLUTION: Either ask if someone else has a different answer or ask additional questions that will cause the right answer to emerge. As the women get closer to the right answer, say, "We're getting warmer! Keep thinking! We're almost there!"

Learning from Experience

Immediately after each Bible study session, evaluate the group discussion time using this checklist. You may also want a member of your group (or an assistant or trainee or outside observer) to evaluate you periodically.

May God strengthen—and encourage!—you as you assist others in the discovery of His many wonderful truths.